5/24

ELEANOR OF AQUITAINE
and the High Middle Ages

by Nancy Plain

Marshall Cavendish
Benchmark
New York

ACKNOWLEDGMENT

The author wishes to specially thank Professor Catherine McKenna, Coordinator of Medieval Studies at the Graduate Center of the City University of New York, for her invaluable help in reading the manuscript.

For Alan,
A "VERRAY PARFIT GENTIL KNIGHT"

Marshall Cavendish Benchmark
99 White Plains Road
Tarrytown, New York 10591-9001
www.marshallcavendish.us

Text copyright © 2006 by Miriam Greenblatt
Map copyright © 2006 by Marshall Cavendish Corporation
Map by Rodica Prato

All Internet sites were available and accurate when this book was sent to press.

Library of Congress Cataloging-in-Publication Data
Plain, Nancy.
Eleanor of Aquitaine and the High Middle Ages / by Nancy Plain.
p. cm. — (Rulers and their times)
Includes bibliographical references and index.
ISBN 0-7614-1834-2
1. Eleanor, of Aquitaine, Queen, consort of Henry II, King of England, 1122?–1204—Juvenile literature. 2. Great Britain—History—Henry II, 1154–1189—Biography—Juvenile literature. 3. France—History—Louis VII, 1137–1180—Biography—Juvenile literature. 4. Queens—Great Britain—Biography—Juvenile literature. 5. Queens—France—Biography—Juvenile literature. 6. Middle Ages—Juvenile literature. I. Title. II. Series.
DA209.E6P58 2005   942.03'1'092—dc22   2004000033
Art Research: Rose Corbett Gordon, Mystic CT
Cover: The Art Archive / Dagli Orti
Page i: British Library/Bridgeman Art Library; pages 2, 11, 43, 68, 69, 70, 75, 79, 83, 86: The Granger Collection, New York; pages 5, 63, 85: Erich Lessing/Art Resource, NY; pages 8–9: The Art Archive/Biblioteca Nazionale Turin/Dagli Orti; page 14: The Art Archive/Basilique Saint Denis Paris/Dagli Orti; pages 17, 46–47: The Art Archive/Real biblioteca de lo Escorial/Dagli Orti; pages 19, 66–67: Bibliotheque Nationale, Paris/Bridgeman Art Library; page 22: Private Collection/Bridgeman Art Library; page 24: Universitatsbibliothek, Heidelberg, Germany/Bridgeman Art Library; page 26: Giraudon/Art Resource, NY; pages 29, 56: British Library/Topham-HIP/The Image Works; page 31: Reunion des Musées Nationaux/Art Resource, NY; page 33: Yale Center for British Art, Paul Mellon Fund, USA/Bridgeman Art Library; page 36: The Art Archive/Dagli Orti; page 39: Topham/The Image Works; page 40: The Art Archive/British Museum; page 48: The Art Archive/Biblioteca Estense Modena/Dagli Orti; pages 51, 82: The Art Archive/British Library; page 53: Glasgow University Library, Scotland/Bridgeman Art Library; page 57: Snark/Art Resource, NY; page 60: Lee Snider/The Image Works; page 73: Arxiu de la Paeria, Lleida, Catalunya, Spain/Index/Bridgeman Art Library; page 78: AKG, London.

Printed in China
135642

Permission has been granted to use extended quotations from the following copyrighted works:

Arthurian Romances by Chrétien de Troyes. Translated by William W. Kibler. Translation copyright © William W. Kibler. London: Penguin Classics, 1991, pp. 276–277. Reprinted by permission of Penguin Books Ltd.

Letters of the Queens of England, edited by Anne Crawford. Gloucestershire: Sutton Publishing Limited, 1994, pp. 39–41 [Foedera, vol. 1, pp. 74–76, Latin]. Reprinted by permission of Sutton Publishing Ltd.

Contents

The Destiny of a Duchess

In Europe long ago, in the year 1122, when stone castles towered over the land and knights jousted to the clang of lance upon shield, a girl named Eleanor was born. As the eldest child of Duke William X of Aquitaine, she inherited the richest domain in France—and all of Europe. She could have lived forever as a duchess in her family's palaces, amid vineyards and meadows and rivers that sparkled in the sun. But a more brilliant future awaited her.

At fifteen, she married the pious young man who would become Louis VII, king of France. But the marriage was not a happy one. "I thought to have married a king, but find I have married a monk," Eleanor complained, and after fifteen years as Louis's queen, she obtained a divorce. As soon as she was free, Eleanor married the restless and bold Henry Plantagenet, who as Henry II would go down in history as one of England's greatest kings. Uniting England and all their lands in France, Eleanor and Henry crafted the Angevin Empire, the largest and mightiest empire in the Europe of its day. They also started the Plantagenet dynasty, which would supply England with eight kings, one of whom was Richard the Lionheart, Eleanor's favorite son.

Eleanor of Aquitaine lived during medieval times, or the Middle Ages. This was the era that began after the fall of the Roman

This is the beautiful stone effigy on Eleanor of Aquitaine's tomb. The medieval sculptor placed a book in the queen's hands to symbolize her love of poetry and learning.

Empire, in the late 400s, and ended in the 1400s, as the Renaissance began. The Middle Ages lasted for one thousand years. Those ten centuries—violent, superstitious, creative, and spiritual—were the long journey that brought Western civilization to the brink of the modern age.

In medieval times, there were no nations as we think of them today. Most of Europe was a patchwork of feudal territories, or fiefs, ruled by wealthy lords, such as kings, dukes, or counts. These lords would, in turn, parcel out their land to lesser nobles, or vassals, in return for military service and feudal dues. In ceremonies of homage, vassals vowed loyalty to their lords. But vows were often broken, and vassals sometimes conquered more territory even than their king, who was technically overlord of them all. "Might makes right" seems to have been the motto that guided feudal politics. Eleanor and all the lords she knew lived in a state of constant warfare.

Eleanor's century, coming toward the end of the period, was part of the High Middle Ages. It was a time of great events and achievements. During her long life, which ended in 1204, Eleanor took part in or witnessed firsthand many of them.

When she was queen of France, she saw the first church to be built in the miraculous Gothic style, and she accompanied King Louis to Jerusalem on the Second Crusade. As queen of England, Eleanor helped carry out Henry's revolutionary program to bring about justice and the rule of law. On her own, she encouraged a new art form called troubadour poetry. And she perfected the concept of "courtly love," aspects of which are very much alive today.

In an age when women were expected to stay in the background, Eleanor dared to divorce a king, forge an empire, and apply her extraordinary political skill for the benefit of her sons. In acting as she pleased, she made enemies. She was called "a very evil woman" and even inspired a baseless rumor that she had poisoned a rival. She was also said to have been extremely beautiful. Although we will never know what she looked like, a poet of her day called her "gracious, lovely, the embodiment of charm."

Eight hundred years have come and gone since Eleanor of Aquitaine lived. The chroniclers who recorded the history of their day left out many details, so much of Eleanor's life remains a mystery. But one thing is certain: she was one of the most remarkable women ever to wear a crown.

PART ONE

The history of Europe would have turned out quite differently without Eleanor of Aquitaine. Yet we know nothing about her appearance, not even the color of her hair. But she and her two royal husbands certainly wore fur-trimmed robes like the ones shown in this painting from a medieval manuscript.

Eleanor, the Queen

Queen of France

When Eleanor was fifteen, her father, Duke William X of Aquitaine, died. It then became the duty of her overlord, France's King Louis VI—also known as Louis the Fat—to find the young duchess a husband. Although the king himself was dying, he knew exactly what to do. He chose his own sixteen-year-old son, Louis, who was heir to the French throne.

It did not matter that Eleanor and Louis the Young had never met. In the blazing hot summer of 1137, in the city of Bordeaux, they were married. Almost as soon as the bride had changed out of her magnificent red wedding robe, the new couple began the journey back to the king's palace, in Paris. But by the time they arrived, Louis the Fat was already dead. Eleanor was now queen of France, and her husband was Louis VII, a monarch of the long-lasting Capetian dynasty.

France in the Middle Ages was divided into feudal provinces called duchies and counties. The only part of the country actually called "France" then was the king's small domain. It consisted of Paris and the surrounding area, known as the Île-de-France, and the people who lived there were called Franks. Louis felt lucky to have married Eleanor: not only was she beautiful, but as Duchess of Aquitaine and Countess of Poitou, she possessed far more land than he.

Aquitaine. Because it bordered the sea and was laced with rivers,

King Louis VII, surrounded here by his advisers, was thought by many who knew him to be better suited for the life of a bishop than that of a king.

it was named by the Romans to mean "land of waters." Eleanor's realm, which included the county of Poitou to the north, spanned the central and southwestern part of the country—about one-quarter of present-day France. One medieval chronicler wrote that Aquitaine was "sweet as nectar . . . one of the happiest and most fertile among the provinces." There was fishing and trade along its Atlantic coast; wine making in the south; and forests, fruit trees, and farms almost everywhere.

Eleanor's childhood home was the ancestral family palace in the city of Poitiers. There, according to one who knew her, she

Ireland

Scotland

England

Wales

NORTH
SEA

London •
Canterbury •
Salisbury •

Flanders

The Holy
ROMAN
EMPIRE

ENGLISH CHANNEL

ATLANTIC

OCEAN

Rouen •

Normandy

Vexin
Paris •

Champagne

Blois

Île-de-France

Brittany

Maine

Angers •
Fontevrault •
Anjou

Touraine
Chinon •

Berry

Poitou

Mirebeau •
Poitiers •

Limoges •

Aquitaine

Bordeaux •

N

Castile

PYRENEES

MEDITERRANEAN
SEA

*France and England in the time of
Eleanor of Aquitaine*

——— Angevin Empire

0   50   100 mi

grew up "with abundance of all delights, living in the bosom of wealth." Her grandfather, Duke William IX, was France's first known troubadour poet; Eleanor was brought up in the family tradition of love for literature and music. Perhaps she also took after her grandmother, an adventurous countess named Dangereuse (Dangerous). The chroniclers noted that Eleanor was "lively" and "charming." She was also supremely confident, and she had a taste for luxury and pleasure.

Louis VII did not. The tall, blond youth saved most of his passion for religion. He had been trained for high office in the Church and had inherited the throne only because his eldest brother had died.

Trying too hard to prove himself a strong king, Louis got off to a bad start. He quarreled with one of his most powerful vassals, Count Thibaut of Champagne, and in 1143 invaded Thibaut's county. As Louis's soldiers slashed their way through Champagne, they came to a little town called Vitry. Its citizens ran to their church for protection. But the church was torched, and everyone inside burned to death. Louis saw it all. The sound—and the horrible smell—of the massacre drove him nearly crazy with guilt. When he returned to Eleanor in Paris, she found she could do nothing to stop his nightmares.

One year after Vitry, Louis and Eleanor attended one of the most important events of their time: the dedication ceremony of the abbey church of Saint-Denis. The church had been redesigned under the guiding genius of a prelate named Abbot Suger, and it was a masterpiece in the Gothic style, the first of its kind. Its soaring arches and jewel-colored windows were an expression of the deep Christian faith held by most medieval Europeans, a faith

as natural to them as the air they breathed. At Saint-Denis, Louis prayed for forgiveness for the massacre. Still, he could find no peace of mind.

Eleanor was unhappy, too. Although she gave birth to a daughter, Marie, in 1145, she had not yet produced a son to inherit Louis's throne. Worse, she had little in common with a husband who was sunk in gloom. But soon both king and queen would have a dramatic chance to make a new start. It was called *Crusade*.

Opposite: The wise and learned Abbot Suger was chief adviser to King Louis VI and also supervised the education of the king's son. But when the boy became Louis VII and married Eleanor of Aquitaine, Suger lost much of his influence over royal affairs. He then turned his brilliant mind to the development of Gothic architecture.

Crusade

Palestine, that small piece of land on the eastern shore of the Mediterranean Sea, had been in Arab hands since the 600s. Medieval Europeans, almost all of whom were Christians, called it the Holy Land. It was the setting of many stories told in the Bible; Christians made pilgrimages to Palestine to see where Jesus Christ had lived and died.

In the 1000s, a Muslim people called the Seljuk Turks invaded the Mediterranean region. By 1071, they controlled the Holy Land, including the historic city of Jerusalem. Unlike the Arabs, the Seljuks did not tolerate pilgrims. When Europeans heard that numbers of Christian travelers were being enslaved and even murdered by the Turks, they launched the First Crusade.

Lasting from 1096 to 1099, it was a sweeping, if temporary, success. European armies defeated the Turks and established in the Middle East four Christian "kingdoms": Edessa, Antioch, Tripoli, and Jerusalem.

But in 1144, the Turks struck again and conquered Edessa. Abbot Bernard of Clairvaux, one of the most influential prelates of his day, traversed Europe, preaching the need for another crusade. He convinced tens of thousands of men to fight. Women volunteered also, to show their support. "To Jerusalem!" the crowds shouted. "God wills it!" For Louis, here was a way at last to obtain God's pardon for the burning of Vitry. Eleanor, too,

Knights rode on a total of eight crusades to the Middle East, from the eleventh to the thirteenth century. One particularly disastrous crusade, in 1212, was composed entirely of children. A positive effect of these campaigns, however, was the exchange of trade goods and knowledge between European and Middle Eastern cultures.

was caught up in the desire to do great deeds.

The Second Crusade set out in June 1147. Eleanor and Louis led an immense army. In addition to thousands of foot soldiers, there were lords and ladies from every province in France, knights and bishops, peasants, beggars, even outlaws. Some crusaders had joined to serve God, some to grab loot, and some to escape hunger and trouble at home. The procession of people, weapons, horses, pack mules, and baggage carts wound its way south through Europe. With acrobats and jugglers providing entertainment, it resembled a giant parade; everyone was in a festive mood.

But not for long. Within weeks, the army faced food shortages. Soldiers began to desert. And Louis found himself struggling to keep order. As they marched, the crusaders grew weary. In October, they stopped to rest in the richest city in the medieval world—Constantinople.

This was the capital of the Byzantine Empire, the Christian extension of the Roman Empire that was founded in A.D. 330. For some time, the Byzantines had been losing territory. Recently, the Seljuk Turks had taken much of the empire's land in Asia Minor (present-day Turkey). Although the Byzantine emperor, Manuel Comnenus, wanted Louis to help him fight the Turks, he was still wary of the French king's large and unruly army. He urged the crusaders to move on. Eleanor stayed just long enough to compare the emperor's exercise of absolute power with her husband's weak leadership. Louis could not even stop his men from plundering the towns through which he marched, even though he punished the disobedient soldiers by having their hands and ears cut off.

Leaving Constantinople, the crusaders headed to the city of Antioch. Their route took them through the dangerous wilderness

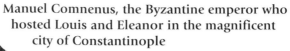

Manuel Comnenus, the Byzantine emperor who hosted Louis and Eleanor in the magnificent city of Constantinople

of Asia Minor, and as one man wrote, "their horses' hooves trod the very floor of hell." In a mountain pass, Louis's forces were ambushed. The king and queen escaped the Turks' arrows, but hundreds of soldiers died. Coming down from the mountain, starving survivors were forced to eat their horses and mules. Then there was an outbreak of plague.

Eleanor and Louis, and all who were able to, reached Antioch in March 1148. The city, second only to Constantinople in splendor, was ruled by Eleanor's uncle, Prince Raymond. He welcomed the crusaders with exotic fruits and wine, then urged Louis to attack Edessa and free it from the Turks. But the king refused. He would make no further plans until he had been to Jerusalem to pray. At this point, Eleanor lost all hope for the success of the crusade. Over the past months, she had lost respect for Louis as well. She told him that she wanted to stay in Antioch with her uncle Raymond. And she told him that she wanted a divorce, using an excuse common in medieval times: she and Louis were, in truth, distantly related to each other. Therefore, their marriage was unlawful in the eyes of God.

Louis begged Eleanor to wait before seeking to break up their marriage. He dreaded losing her. For as one chronicler observed, the king "loved the queen passionately, in an almost childish way." Anxious to tear his wife away from Antioch, anxious to see the holy shrines in Jerusalem, Louis gathered together his army in the darkness of night. Swiftly, he seized Eleanor, ignoring her fury, and forced her to accompany him and his men to Jerusalem.

Once in the ancient city, the royal couple barely spoke to each other. But Louis and his advisers were busy plotting their next military move. That summer of 1148, the crusaders lost a decisive battle against the Muslim city of Damascus, and the Second Crusade finally fell apart.

Louis and Eleanor were the last of the crusaders to return to Paris. Back home, the king faced the shame of his defeat in battle. He also faced the possibility of losing his wife—and with her, the rich land of Aquitaine.

Great Henry

In 1150, the monarchs' second daughter, Alix, was born. Thirteen years of marriage and the king only had two children of the "lesser sex," as he referred to girls. Could this be, as Eleanor had said, a sign of God's anger? Now even Louis considered divorce.

The royal marriage was annulled on March 21, 1152. Louis kept custody of their daughters but was required to return to Eleanor the duchy of Aquitaine.

Two months later, Eleanor shocked the world by marrying again. Her new husband was the red-haired Henry Plantagenet, Duke of Normandy and Count of Maine and Anjou. (*Plantagenet* was a nickname first given to Henry's father, Count Geoffrey of Anjou, who wore a sprig of the *planta genesta*, or broom plant, tucked into his hat.)

Henry was only eighteen years old to Eleanor's thirty, but he was already a powerful lord. Forceful, hot-tempered, and a whirlwind of energy, he was ambitious enough for ten men. In marrying Eleanor, he acquired Aquitaine, too. Now, with Plantagenet lands stretching from Normandy in the north to Aquitaine in the south, Henry was much richer in land and treasure than King Louis. For Louis, this surprise marriage was the worst betrayal of his life.

Henry also had a claim to the English throne, as a grandson of England's King Henry I. But after the old king's death, another claimant, Stephen of Blois, had snatched the crown. Soon after his wedding, young Henry rushed off with his knights to invade England.

While her husband fought, Eleanor established her court in the city of Angers, capital of Henry's ancestral county of Anjou. Here in the green valley of the Loire River, she began her new life. She felt like a bird set free from a cage. She invited to her castle friends and family members from Poitiers. And she surrounded herself with troubadours, those courtly poets who, beginning

Nobles dance against a background of the broom plant, or *planta genesta*, which gave Henry II's family its last name.

with her grandfather, had developed their art in the south of France, and whose beautiful verse was sung to the sweet music of tambourine and strings.

Before the coming of the troubadours, most French poetry was written to celebrate heroic warriors mowing down their enemies in battle. But the new poets sang of love. Troubadours took their inspiration from many places: the poetry of ancient Greece and Rome, Arabic literature, and even from the Christian practice of worshipping the Virgin Mary. The strands of influence were diverse, but the poets' underlying theme was always the same: "courtly love," a kind of romance that often involved a knight who put his lady on a pedestal and was content to adore her from afar.

One of the finest poets Eleanor welcomed to Angers was Bernard de Ventadour. He was enchanted with the young queen. His poems describe her "lovely eyes and noble countenance," and thoughts of her, he wrote, were like a "breath of paradise." A great many other troubadours, too, wrote about Henry's bride. She became their greatest patron and helped to spread their art throughout Europe.

As happy as she was in the Loire Valley, Eleanor did not stay there long. Henry's struggles in England had proven wildly successful; he had won the right to inherit the throne. So when Stephen of Blois died in 1154, twenty-one-year-old Henry, who was already back on the Continent when he heard the news, became Henry II, England's first Plantagenet king. He and Eleanor sailed triumphantly across the English Channel. In a splendid candlelit ceremony in London's Westminster Abbey, the two new monarchs were crowned. Now the couple's empire—called "Angevin" because it had originated in Anjou—reached from the

This is the type of entertainment that Eleanor often enjoyed: a singer, who may also have been a poet, accompanied by the music of fiddle and flute.

boundary of Scotland to the foothills of the Pyrenees Mountains, bordering Spain.

Stephen's reign had left England starving and crime-ridden. The new king was hailed hopefully as "Henry the Peacemaker."

He was. He loved justice and order. Immediately he set to work establishing the unified rule of law in a country where before only local courts—and superstition—had held sway. To apply his laws, Henry appointed judges to travel regularly to the king's courts throughout the land. Before Henry's reign, many legal cases had been settled by "ordeals." In an ordeal by fire, the accused was made to walk over red-hot pieces of iron. If he was badly burned, it was taken as a sign from God that he was guilty. Noblemen were sometimes judged by ordeal by combat. Those who won their fight were deemed innocent. Henry gradually replaced these customs with the system of trial by jury—verdicts decided by "twelve good men and true." Thus, "Great Henry" planted the seeds of English common law: the tradition of justice for which England is famous, and the basis of the British and American legal systems today.

To run his wide empire, constantly disrupted by warring vassals, Henry raced back and forth between England and his lands on the European continent, those duchies and counties that today make up much of modern France. He moved so fast that even Louis VII remarked that the English king "seems rather to come on wings than by horse or boat."

When Henry was away from England, Eleanor acted as regent, ruling in his place. Journeying from one royal castle to another, she carried out the king's orders, tended to financial matters, and settled legal disputes. Even when pregnant, she seldom slowed

The seal of King Henry II of England, emblem of his reign

down. On official documents her name is signed with a regal flourish: "Eleanor, by the Grace of God, Queen of England."

In just a few years, Henry and Eleanor had built an empire that changed the political map of Europe. They had also—to Louis's dismay—created a family with plenty of sons. Their first child, William, died at the age of three, but between 1155 and 1166, seven other babies were born: Henry, Matilda, Richard, Geoffrey, Eleanor, Joanna, and John. It seemed that everything the Plantagenets touched turned to gold.

Trouble in the Kingdom

As helpful as Eleanor was to Henry, there was someone he trusted more—his chancellor, Thomas Becket. Becket was the king's chief administrator, performing many duties that Henry preferred to ignore. He showered Thomas with money and gifts and gave him an elegant mansion in London, where the chancellor lavishly entertained England's leading lords. Becket traveled everywhere with Henry, too, as the king labored to unite his empire under a centralized government. In leisure, as well, the two men were inseparable. One eyewitness remembered, "The King and Becket played together like little boys of the same age, at the court, in church, in assemblies, in riding." Eleanor may have been jealous, but there is no record of her complaints.

In 1162, Henry promoted Becket to the post of archbishop of Canterbury, head of the Church in England. The king expected his friend's help in reining in the power of the Church. Most especially, Henry wanted to end what he considered an outrageous abuse of power—the Church's practice of trying, in its own courts, clerks accused of crimes. ("Clerks" were not always priests or monks; they could be anyone who worked for, or was educated in, the Church.) Since religious courts handed out light sentences, some clerks were literally getting away with murder. Would Becket agree to send these criminals to the king's *civil* courts for sentencing?

To Henry's amazement, Thomas said "No." He would obey the monarch in all other things, he explained, but he would not weaken the authority of the Church, nor offend the "honor of God." In his new role, Becket had changed almost instantly from a worldly man who loved luxury to a pious one who slept on the floor and washed the feet of the poor. He would no longer serve the king in his battle for control over the Church. Henry could not understand this sudden independence. "Aren't you the son of a peasant of mine?" he screamed at Thomas.

Henry was determined to have his way. In 1164, he presented to his council a list of sixteen legal reforms that he intended to make. These Constitutions of Clarendon placed the Church under royal control, an important step in what would be a long struggle between Church and State. They were also a unique moment in English history: the first time ever that a king had put any laws into writing.

Becket would not back down. Instead he fled to Paris, where King Louis gave him refuge. When Henry found out, he had one of his famous tantrums, tearing off his clothes, shrieking, and chewing the straw of his mattress!

Becket was not Henry's only problem. The king spent much of the 1160s repelling attacks on the Angevin Empire. He battled King Louis in the Vexin, a wedge of land on the border between Normandy and the Île-de-France that was an eternal source of conflict between the two kings. He fought rebellious vassals in the county of Maine. And he galloped furiously with his knights through Aquitaine, whose barons hated him for limiting their freedom.

In this illustration from a medieval text, Henry II seems to be lecturing Thomas Becket. When he was appointed archbishop of Canterbury, Becket had predicted trouble in his relationship with the king.

Meanwhile, Louis's fortunes were changing. He had had two more daughters with his second wife, Constance, before she died. But in 1165, his third wife, Adele of Champagne, gave birth to a son. The baby's name was Philip Augustus, but the French joyfully called him Dieu-Donné, or "God-Given."

The Plantagenets worried: would little "God-Given" grow up to threaten their lands on the Continent? In 1169, at the castle of Montmirail, Henry divided his kingdom among his sons—an arrangement that he hoped would safeguard their futures after his death. Lord Henry, the eldest, was to rule Normandy, Anjou, and Maine. Richard received Aquitaine, as Eleanor wished. Geoffrey was to be Count of Brittany, a province Henry had controlled since 1158. Only John, the youngest, was promised nothing. And long before Montmirail, Henry had named his son Henry as the next king of England. To ensure this claim, the "Young King" was crowned in 1170. It was only a token crown, though, since the father granted the fifteen-year-old boy no real power.

In 1170, too, Henry tried to make peace with Thomas Becket and invited him back to his post at Canterbury Cathedral. But once the archbishop was in England, the strife between the two men continued, until one day when Henry is said to have bellowed, "Who will rid me of this turbulent priest?"

On December 29, 1170, four knights loyal to Henry burst into Canterbury Cathedral. According to a monk who was there, the men dragged Becket from prayer and hacked at his head with their swords until Thomas's blood and brains spilled out on the floor.

Whatever Henry had shouted in anger, he had not meant to order Becket's murder. When he heard about it, he fell into a frenzy of sorrow and regret. To no avail. His reputation in Europe, and even in his family, was badly damaged because of this crime. And it would never fully recover.

"Who will rid me of this turbulent priest?" The murder of Thomas Becket raised the pious cleric to sainthood and brought a repentant Henry to his knees.

Courtly Love and Rebellion

Well before the death of Becket, Eleanor's feelings for Henry had begun to cool. Perhaps she was angry at the attention her husband was paying to Rosamund Clifford, a lovely young woman whose first name meant "Rose of the World." Or perhaps Eleanor craved an independence that was hard to achieve as Henry's queen. In 1167, she decided to live apart from him. With several of her children, she sailed away from England and headed to the city of her youth, Poitiers. Henry was not opposed to her going. Aquitaine was the hardest of all his lands to control; he hoped that his wife would be a calming influence among the rebellious barons.

Although still queen of England, Eleanor now concentrated on her role as Duchess of Aquitaine. As duchess, she could use her political skill to a greater extent than ever before. She won a measure of peace from her barons by giving them favors instead of fights. She returned castles that Henry had taken and undid many of his harsher laws. In her peacemaking efforts, twelve-year-old Richard was at her side, for he was her chosen heir.

In the early 1170s, Eleanor reestablished Poitiers as the cultural center it had been under her forebears. Back came philosophers and artists. Once again there were jousting tournaments, and feasts were held in the palace's great hall. Nobles of the younger

An encounter between Queen Eleanor and Henry's new love, the blond-haired Rosamund Clifford, as imagined by a nineteenth-century artist. In the centuries following Eleanor's rule, storytellers spread a tale that the jealous queen poisoned the younger woman, but the two probably never even met.

generation gathered there, and it was home, at various times, to most of the Plantagenet children. There, too, Eleanor renewed her relationship with the eldest daughter of her first marriage, Marie, now Countess of Champagne.

With Marie's help, Eleanor refined and expanded the troubadour concept of courtly love. The queen and her noble ladies formulated a code of conduct, a set of manners designed to civilize rough young knights and teach them to treat women with gentleness and respect. Sometimes the code addressed practical matters, such as what gifts were proper for a man to give a woman. Sometimes its rules were general, as in the instruction to be "obedient in all things to the commands of ladies." More than just an aristocratic pastime, the pursuit of courtly love became a kind of counterbalance to the violence and fury of the male-dominated feudal world. Most radical of all was the fact that Eleanor's ideas were based on her belief that women were actually *superior* to men and that, as such, they had every right to make their own decisions in life. Although these values were only rarely put into practice in Eleanor's day, they became the basis of a kind of medieval women's movement and were eagerly discussed throughout Europe.

As she had at Angers, Eleanor made Poitiers a magnet for the best troubadours in France. And they appreciated her as much as she did them. One chronicler writes that Eleanor "had understanding in matters of valor and honor, and cared for a song of praise." She was to poets, another man wrote, "what dawn is to birds."

But poetry did not consume all of Eleanor's time. There was always politics. Now in her late forties and estranged from her second husband, Eleanor focused on her teenage sons. They were angry that they would have to wait until Henry died to fully control their inherited domains. The Young King, especially, had an empty title. But Henry thought him irresponsible and would give him no authority at all over the lands promised him— England, Normandy, Anjou, and Maine. Eleanor sided with the Young King in bitter family arguments, and her feelings for Henry ripened to hatred. At Poitiers, she plotted with her sons—all except the little boy John—to overthrow Henry II. Incredibly, she teamed up with King Louis, as her overlord in France, to accomplish her goal.

"Beware your wife and sons," Henry was warned. But it was too late. In 1173, the Great Rebellion broke out. All the lords who resented the king's rule also joined the conspiracy, and almost every part of the empire came under attack. Like lightning, however, Henry and his armies tore through the realm, burning and killing without mercy. In just one year, he stamped out all revolts in England and the Continent. Louis withdrew his men, and the Plantagenet sons were forced to accept peace.

Meanwhile, Eleanor had disguised herself as a knight and tried to flee to Paris. But she was captured, and in the summer of 1174, the king imprisoned her in Salisbury Tower, in England. As a royal prisoner, the queen was treated rather well. She was permitted to keep a servant and was occasionally supplied with new furs and cloaks. Her real punishment lay in the fact that there in the dark fortress, she was cut off from the world and from the sons for whom she had gambled everything.

Henry still withheld power from his eldest son, and the Young King was mocked as "lord of little land." As the years passed, he became increasingly jealous of his younger brother Richard, who

This wall painting was uncovered in a chapel in France, in 1964. Historians believe that the scene depicts Eleanor being led into captivity after the failure of her revolt against Henry.

was now ruling Aquitaine on behalf of his mother. In 1183, the Young King and his brother Geoffrey joined a widespread revolt against Richard. Henry tried to negotiate with his eldest son, but as a chronicler put it, "War was in his heart." That summer, in the midst of rampaging through Richard's land, the Young King caught a fever and died.

The messenger who broke the news to Henry wrote that the king "threw himself upon the ground and greatly bewailed his son." In her tenth year of imprisonment, Eleanor also heard the news. But she already knew her son was dead, she said. She had seen it in a dream.

Richard the Lionheart

This was Bernard of Clairvaux's prophecy for the Plantagenets: "From the devil they came, to the devil they will go." They *were* a family torn apart by lust for power. Even after the Young King died, the brothers continued to fight. Eighteen-year-old John now joined Geoffrey in battling Richard in Poitou. And Henry decided to undo the provisions of Montmirail; making promises to his sons had caused too much trouble. In 1184, he asked Richard to give Aquitaine to John. Naturally, Richard refused, because the domain he had received from his mother was the place he loved best on earth. The king then forced Eleanor to take back the duchy from her son so that Henry could bring it under his control. Two years later, Geoffrey died in a jousting accident. Of all the sons, only Richard and John were left.

Family troubles aside, Henry also had to deal with Louis's son, who had been crowned Philip II, king of France, in 1179. (King Louis had died in 1180, one year after putting Philip on the throne.) The shrewd Philip was intent on breaking up the Angevin Empire. In the late 1180s, he repeatedly invaded the Vexin and parts of the duchy of Berry. Henry fought back.

Betraying his father for the second time, Richard joined Philip's side. Why such disloyalty? Again and again, Richard, now the eldest son, had asked Henry to name him heir to England and to give him control of his provinces on the Continent. Again and again, Henry had refused.

In 1189, the armies of Philip and Richard were seizing Henry's cities and fortresses in central France. Henry, overwhelmed and sick, took refuge in his castle of Chinon, in Anjou. "My whole body is on fire," he groaned. Soon he was forced to surrender. Richard demanded his father's entire realm—immediately—and the humiliated king had to agree.

Then came the final blow. Henry learned that John, too, had fought against him. "Say no more," he cried. "Now let the rest go as it will. I care no more for myself, nor for aught in this world." For thirty-five years, Henry II had ruled with a shining vision of justice and government, but he died on July 6, 1189, thinking himself a failure. In his last agony, he called out, "Shame, shame on a conquered king!"

The tall, red-haired Richard showed no grief. The empire was finally his, and he was prepared to hold it together. For he was the fearless "Lionheart," more ruthless in war even than his father. His mother called him "the great one."

When Henry died, Eleanor was set free. She was sixty-seven and had been a prisoner for sixteen years. In all that time, she had lost none of her energy and dignity. She now applied her talent for public relations to one thing: Richard's happy coronation as king of England. Even before he arrived in the country, she won good-will for him. She built a hospital, freed prisoners, issued new coins for the realm. During this period, the queen earned a reputation for "great wisdom" as her son's regent and came to be "exceedingly respected and beloved."

Henry II, who built an empire, founded a dynasty, and planted the seeds of the English legal system, died betrayed by his own sons.

King Richard I was crowned on September 3, 1189. But he would spend little time governing England. Crusade fever was spreading through Europe once again.

In 1187, the Turkish leader Saladin had conquered Jerusalem and captured its Christian king. Horrified at the news, both Richard and Philip vowed to free the Holy Land. They began the Third Crusade in 1190, with an army so huge that, it was said, "The Earth trembled with its coming."

By 1191, the crusaders were at the walls of the Turkish-controlled port of Acre, near Jerusalem. They attacked the city with battering rams, flaming missiles, and crossbows. The English king's assault was so savage that the Turks called him "Evil Richard."

Acre surrendered. But malaria was now infecting the crusaders' ranks. Soldiers deserted or died by the thousands. Philip gave up and went home. And Richard knew that there were not enough soldiers left to free Jerusalem. Sadly, he signed a truce with Saladin and, in 1192, sailed for France.

On the way, he was captured by an enemy and handed over to Henry VI, the Holy Roman Emperor, who held him prisoner. Eleanor's reaction to this was utter despair. She wrote letters to

Richard the Lionheart *(left)* **and Saladin, who fought each other during the Third Crusade, were two of the most feared warriors of their time.**

Pope Celestine III, begging him to help free her son. Without Richard, her life was "torment," and she told the pope, "I long for death." But then, with typical determination, she raised an enormous ransom and, in 1194, obtained Richard's release.

During the Lionheart's long absence, Philip had raided Angevin lands from Normandy to Aquitaine. Now that Richard was back, he would spend the rest of his reign locked in combat with Philip, as the two kings vied for control of France.

Endless warfare had left Richard in dire need of money. In 1199, he heard that a treasure of gold coins had been found in a field and locked away in a castle near the city of Limoges. He besieged the castle in order to obtain the gold. But he was shot in the arm with an arrow, and the wound became badly infected. Eleanor rode—practically flew—one hundred miles to be at Richard's side. She was there on April 6, when he died, this son whom she called "the staff of my old age, the light of my eyes."

King John

John, Eleanor's last surviving son, had a reputation for being "light-minded." At thirty-three, he was also lazy, selfish, unreliable, and conniving. While Richard was in captivity, John had plotted with Philip to undermine the Angevin Empire. Now that the realm was his, however, Philip would become his deadliest enemy. Eleanor put aside her grief over Richard and concentrated on securing John's future. She made sure that he was quickly declared Duke of Normandy and, in May 1199, crowned king of England.

But Philip was relentless. He formed an alliance with Arthur of Brittany, the teenage son of John's dead brother Geoffrey. (Arthur was also Eleanor's grandson.) Philip proclaimed Arthur to be the rightful heir to the empire. He gave the boy an army, and their combined forces invaded the Plantagenet domain. Eleanor and John fought back, but even Aquitaine and Poitou remained under threat.

Eleanor refused to act like an old woman. She embarked on a one-thousand-mile journey through Aquitaine in order to gain support for the ongoing struggle with the king of France. Her trip was a healing mission. She bestowed gifts, heard petitions, and judged disputes. Then, a stroke of genius: she granted independence to many towns, freeing them from their feudal ties. These liberated towns would now defend *themselves* in warfare. More importantly, they would become home to the new, growing

King John, pictured here on a white horse, was Eleanor's least favorite son. He is remembered for signing, in 1215, the Magna Carta. The famous document, in which the king gave up some of his power to the nobility, laid the foundation for English democracy.

middle class of citizens who, without feudal obligations, would gradually change the face of Europe. By Christmas 1199, Philip and John were at a standoff. They signed a truce. They even arranged for one of Eleanor's granddaughters to marry Philip's son, Prince Louis. So Eleanor, now eighty, traveled to the kingdom of Castile, in Spain, where her daughter Eleanor was queen. There she chose her granddaughter, the pretty and intelligent Blanche of Castile, to marry the French prince. It must have been strange for the elderly Eleanor to think of this girl one day sharing the throne of another King Louis.

This was Eleanor's last long trip. She returned to the abbey of Fontevrault, in Anjou, where she had been living for the past several years. "I have been very ill," she wrote to John, yet she still kept a sharp eye on her troubled empire.

The truce did not last. Philip made another attempt to conquer Angevin lands. In April 1202, he marched into Normandy and directed Arthur to invade Poitou. Eleanor and her soldiers rushed to defend her city of Poitiers, but on the way, they were forced to take refuge at the castle of Mirebeau. There they were about to be captured by Arthur's men when John's army swept down on the castle. John rescued his mother and took many prisoners, including his nephew Arthur.

After the year 1203, Arthur was never seen again. Many believe that John himself murdered him. Rumors of murder, as well as John's brutal treatment of his other prisoners, caused many of his allies to switch to the French side. Angevin cities began to fall like dominoes. And John lost his will to fight: "Let me alone, let me alone. When the time comes I will shortly recover all I have lost." He retreated to England, and within a year, Philip II took possession of Anjou, Maine, Touraine, Brittany, and Normandy. In 1205, he would even take Poitou.

On April 1, 1204, in the midst of all the chaos, Queen Eleanor died. Her death was quiet, says a chronicler, "as a candle goeth out." She had outlived two husbands and all but two of her ten children. As her life ended, so did the empire that she had worked so hard to build.

Epilogue

Eleanor was buried in the tranquil abbey church at Fontevrault, next to Henry II and her beloved Richard. The graceful stone effigy on her tomb gives no hint of the turmoil and passion of her eighty-two years.

She was a fitting ruler for those days of knights in armor, because her life, too, was a quest. She found much of what she sought: beauty in troubadour poetry, respect for women in the code of courtly love, and power in the empire for which she had risked her freedom. Although at her death the Plantagenets' future seemed grim, it was not so. Eleanor's descendants would continue to rule England for the next 250 years. And beginning with a great-grandson, they would also become kings of France. The little Duchess of Aquitaine had grown up to be a queen whose ambitions and beliefs influenced all of Europe. She was one of the most daring figures of her century. The English called her "the Eagle."

PART TWO

For medieval lords, land meant wealth and power. For peasants, land meant endless toil. Here a laborer teaches his son to plow, just as his own father had once taught him.

Everyday Life in Eleanor's Realm

Clothes

In medieval times, most people were peasants. They did not have the luxury of being fussy about their clothes. For backbreaking work in the fields, men dressed in belted tunics, worn over leggings or loose trousers. Caps or hats with wide brims protected them a bit from sun and rain. Peasant women, laboring in cottage as well as field, wore plain, long dresses. Their head coverings were called wimples, similar to what many nuns wear today. The poorest people often went barefoot or made their own wooden clogs, but contemporary tapestries and illustrations also depict bootlike shoes that rose to ankle height or higher. In the frozen winter, peasants wrapped heavy

European peasants wore the same type of clothing for centuries, made from heavy homespun wool or linen.

cloaks around their shoulders. The only other way to stay warm was to huddle inside by the fire, which these laborers were usually far too busy to do.

Wool and linen were most commonly used for clothing. Most women, including the richest, knew how to spin and weave. In Eleanor's day, the production of cloth became a well-organized industry that employed both men and women in countryside and town. England was especially famous for its wool. Its manufacture was a painstaking process, from the shearing of the sheep to the final stage of dyeing the fabric for color. Linen making was profitable, too. That material was used not only for headdresses and tunics; everyone in the Middle Ages wore linen underwear.

When feudal lords and ladies chose wool or linen, it was not rough like the peasants', but soft and supple. And while peasants had been wearing the same type of clothing for centuries, the nobility could afford to dress in the latest style. They loved silk imported from China, garments embroidered with gold thread, jeweled pins to fasten their cloaks. Noblewomen wore sleeves so long that they touched the floor, as well as veils on their heads, held in place by golden circlets. The most expensive cloth was anything dyed the color red.

Nobles from Aquitaine had the reputation of being the most fashion conscious of all, and Eleanor was sometimes criticized for her ornate wardrobe. When she was first married, she shocked Louis's courtiers in Paris with her jewels, perfume, eyeliner, and rouge. As a young woman, she aroused the anger of Abbot Bernard of Clairvaux, whose preaching was to help inspire the Second Crusade. Here he scornfully describes Eleanor and the other women in her circle: "The garments of the court ladies are fashioned from the finest tissues of wool or silk. A costly fur between two layers of rich stuffs forms the lining and border of their cloaks. Their arms are loaded with bracelets; from their ears hang pendants. . . ." Their gowns had long trains that raised the dust as the women walked by, Bernard complained. And he wrote, "Some you see who are not so much adorned as loaded down with gold, silver, and precious stones, and indeed everything that pertains to queenly splendor."

Eleanor made no apology for her love of luxury and display. Like most nobles of her day, she never seems to have wondered at the contrast between her life and that of a peasant's. In the Middle Ages, each person's fate was believed to be determined by God.

Food

"Four-and-twenty blackbirds baked in a pie" was a medieval recipe. The birds could not have been baked for too long, however, for when the pie was opened, they flew around the dining hall, to the amusement of the diners. Some more practical dishes from the era are still popular: *coq au vin* (chicken in wine sauce), omelettes, and *boeuf bourguignon* (a meat-and-red-wine stew). Twelfth-century people ate others kinds of stew, too—even one made of chicken

Nobles held banquets in great halls lit by torches and decorated with banners. Musicians played between courses, and dozens of rich, spicy dishes were served.

entrails, called "garbage." For drinking, the French loved their wine, much of which came from the region around the city of Bordeaux, in Aquitaine. The English were proud of their beer. These beverages were often safer to consume than water. Throughout Europe, bacteria-laden streams and wells at times caused sickness and even death.

Dining customs were less refined than those of today. When Eleanor became queen of France, she surprised the Parisians by bringing tablecloths and napkins to the royal palace. Spoons and knives were commonly used, but not until they visited Constantinople on Crusade were many Europeans introduced to an invention called the *fork*. Even the richest Europeans shared one plate and cup between two people. Peasants had no plates, but piled their food onto thick slices of bread.

Most medieval people ate only what they grew in the narrow little fields that they farmed themselves. They made coarse bread out of wheat, oats, barley, or rye. They grew vegetables, such as peas, onions, turnips, and beans. In Aquitaine, olive trees—prized for the oil the olives yielded—and grapevines were plentiful. Anjou, watered by the Loire River, was called the "fruit basket" of the country. Walnut and apple trees dotted the duchy of Normandy. Whatever the crop, peasants owed a large portion of it to their lord, as payment for using his land.

Peasants usually kept pigs and poultry, a few sheep, and a cow or two. In good times, families consumed dinners of chicken, bacon, cheese, or eggs. But in lean times, after they had eaten their livestock, the poor could starve. They were not permitted to hunt the animals in their lords' forests: this was called poaching, a crime for which a man could be hanged.

Food in the landowners' castles was usually plentiful. Meals were prepared in enormous kitchens, staffed by dozens of servants and equipped with fireplaces large enough to roast whole deer. The main meal was served in midmorning, in the great hall.

At the sound of a trumpet, lords, ladies, knights, and guests sat down at long tables. Squires and pages carried in basins of water for washing and knives to cut the diners' meat. Minstrels, jugglers, and mimes stood ready to entertain.

The nobles ate fish caught in their castle moats and game shot on their land. Roasted fowl, of all kinds, was a favorite. Dessert, an important part of the meal, could be waffles, fruit tarts, macaroons, or gingerbread.

Foods tasted on the Crusades were a great spur

Peasants' most valuable possessions were their livestock. An important source of meat, pigs were especially prized. Here a man feeds acorns to his.

to trade between the Middle East and Europe. In Constantinople, Antioch, and Jerusalem, the French and English discovered figs, dates, raisins, bananas, truffles, and other delicacies. They brought home with them exotic spices to flavor their sauces.

While Poitevins, or people from Poitou, were thought to be "better feeders than fighters," Henry II was comparatively indifferent to food. In an age when a lord's dinner could include at least ten courses, the king of England said, "In my court, I am satisfied with three." He was too busy with his empire to sit eating for very long. Besides, he was afraid of getting fat.

Knights in Armor

"Armed with wood, iron and steel, I shall endure heat, cold, frost; scattered meadows will be my dwelling place. Discords and severities must serve the place of love songs, and I shall maintain the weak against the strong." So wrote one medieval knight. To join the brotherhood of knights, the elite military force of the Middle Ages, he had trained long and hard. He became a lowly page at the age of seven; a squire, or personal assistant to a knight, at fourteen; and finally achieved knighthood himself at twenty-one. Kneeling in a solemn ceremony, he took the sacred vow of chivalry—to serve God, his lord, and his lady.

He would serve God by making his life a heroic quest, or mission, to fulfill Christian ideals, such as going on crusade. He also promised to embrace the religiously inspired values of courtesy, fair play, loyalty, and fighting for the right.

In serving his lord, the knight became an essential part of the feudal system. In exchange for a grant of land, or fief, from the lord, the knight owed forty days of military service. Thus, his lord's enemies became his own. He would ride into battle on a powerful warhorse. He would carry a shield and choose from a variety of weapons: crossbow, sword, battle-ax, or lance. "To be ready for war, a knight . . . must have seen his own blood flow, have had his teeth crackle under the blow of his adversary," wrote one warrior. To withstand this fierce combat, knights wore armor. An

Whether he was besieging a neighboring castle or going on crusade, a knight lived to fight. This warrior, who is taking a vow before going into battle, probably considered it shameful to die peacefully in bed.

early type, called chain mail, consisted of interlocking rings of metal. In the fourteenth century, when the lethal crossbow came into widespread use, stronger armor was needed. Knights began to wear bulkier helmets, with slitlike visors, and body suits made of as many as two hundred iron plates. If a man wearing such heavy armor fell off his horse during a fight, he was probably doomed. Armor was also put on horses and sometimes dogs, to protect them as they hunted wild boar.

Knights practiced their skills at tournaments. In these mock battles (which actually could be quite deadly), two groups of men galloped toward each other with long lances, hoping to "unhorse" their opponents when they collided. When during a tournament only two men faced each other in combat, the game was called "jousting." Eleanor's son the Young King loved to joust. With little else to do, he piled up victories and prize money at tournaments

A king sits in the royal gallery to watch a tournament. This most popular of medieval entertainments was not like the sports of today. Lances could be fourteen feet long, and knights were often killed in the arena, or "tilting ground."

throughout France. Called "the most handsome prince in all the world," he fit perfectly the image of the chivalrous knight.

Tournaments were also glamorous social events. Crowds of spectators sat in brightly colored pavilions that were festooned with banners. Often there was a special throne in the viewing stands for the "Queen of Love and Beauty," the lady judged to be the fairest of the day. Men rode with their ladies' scarves or ribbons tied around their lances. A triumphant knight often claimed his victory in the name of the woman he loved, thus fulfilling the third part of his vow—to serve his lady. Chivalry and courtly love were intertwined.

Castles

The medieval period was the age of castles. Magnificent and forbidding, they sat on the land as if they owned it. And in a sense, they did. They were the headquarters of the great lords' domains, the fortresses from which the powerful controlled their vast holdings. In their castles, rulers lived, kept their treasure and tax revenues, stored their weapons, housed their soldiers, and ran their governments. In times of war, people from the surrounding countryside and towns sought protection behind the castles' walls. These imposing structures were both the symbol and the reality of medieval might.

Henry II spent a fortune building and repairing castles. They were of great strategic importance to him as he struggled to control vassals throughout his empire. Unlike his palaces, which were just large, luxurious residences, the king's castles were strongholds built to withstand the armies of his rivals. Early medieval castles were made of wood, so wherever Henry found these, he replaced them with solid stone.

Most castles were constructed on high points of land that commanded wide views. The typical castle was encircled by a moat, a ditch filled with water. A drawbridge, which could be raised to keep out enemies, led across the moat to the outer wall, or curtain, that enclosed the entire fortress. At the corners of this wall were towers, with windows only wide enough to allow an archer to shoot. On the castle side of the curtain was an open area called the bailey. This was a kind of walled town in itself, with soldiers' barracks, stables, and workshops for armorers and blacksmiths. Beyond another wall was the inner courtyard. Here was the heart of the lord's dwelling—the castle keep.

The keep had to be the safest place in the complex because it

This is the type of castle that Eleanor of Aquitaine might have visited. Built to enclose and protect its inhabitants, it has a moat, massive stone walls, and a tall tower from which to watch for enemies.

contained the great hall, the living quarters of the lord and his family, their servants and staff. The hall was high-ceilinged and spacious, with bright banners hanging from oak rafters and walls decorated with weapons and hunting trophies. Rushes, or grasslike stalks, were strewn on the floor, and a huge fireplace provided warmth.

Privacy was rare in the Middle Ages. The great hall served as dining room and sleeping area for most of the people who lived in the keep. Only the castle's owners had bedrooms of their own.

The great hall was a place of feasting and entertainment. But below the keep, where the underground dungeon was, the lord's prisoners were tortured, or sometimes starved to death. The chivalric ideal of mercy often did not apply to one's enemies.

The strongest fortress on the Continent was Château Gaillard, built by Richard the Lionheart while he was king of England. High above the river Seine, on the border between Normandy and the French territory, the castle was meant to keep Philip II from conquering Normandy and gaining access to the sea. Château Gaillard had three moats. With its advanced system of ditches and walls, it seemed invincible.

When he first saw the castle, Philip boasted, "If its walls were made of solid iron, yet would I take them." But Richard replied, "By the throat of God, if its walls were made of butter, yet would I hold them." The Lionheart did hold Château Gaillard until he died. But in 1204, his brother King John lost it to Philip's men when they tunneled inside through the drainage system. The year Queen Eleanor died, this greatest of Plantagenet strongholds also fell.

Cathedrals

In the Middle Ages, when most people's lives were governed by the whim of a lord instead of the rule of law, the Church served an important stabilizing function. It was the strongest—and often the only—bond that linked the people of Europe. Almost everyone was taught the same doctrines and worshipped in the same way. The Church provided education and gave aid to the poor and the sick. It regulated holidays, held ceremonies for knighthood, and presided over rituals connected with birth, marriage, and death. When medieval men and women were plagued by disease and hunger, the Church gave them comfort. It taught that those who lived by its teachings would receive their reward in heaven, and those who did not risked burning forever in hell.

The kindly Abbot Suger, head of the royal abbey of Saint-Denis, near Paris, believed he knew how to help save souls. "It is only through symbols of beauty that our poor spirits can raise themselves from things temporal to things eternal." Nowhere is this belief more evident than in Suger's marvelous renovation of Saint-Denis.

The church was originally built in the stately Romanesque manner, with thick stone walls and pillars, rounded arches, and small windows with clear glass. Suger assembled scores of craftspeople and laborers to create something different. When the project was finished, in 1144, he unveiled to the public the astonishing new Gothic style.

One of the most spectacular Gothic cathedrals is in Cologne, Germany.

Arches were high and pointed, leading the eye heavenward. Walls could be thinner than before, because flying buttresses, or outside support structures, were helping the walls to hold up the heavy roof. And because thick Romanesque walls were no longer needed, windows could be large. Suger's architects filled them with brilliantly colored stained glass. Making the interior glow, they reflected the medieval idea that God is light. The magical, airy Gothic design set a trend that spread throughout Europe.

Between 1170 and 1270, eighty Gothic cathedrals were constructed in France alone. By the end of the thirteenth century, all new churches in northern Europe were being built in the Gothic style. Three of the finest that can be seen today are in Cologne, Germany; Salisbury, England; and Chartres, France. (The windows of Chartres Cathedral are perhaps the most wonderful in the world.)

Some of the great cathedrals took more than two centuries to complete and required the labor of many hundreds of workers. A master builder was in charge of the entire operation. Then there were men to haul stone, push wheelbarrows, dig foundations. There were skilled artisans: glaziers to make the windows, stone and wood carvers, painters, sculptors, gold- and silversmiths, setters of precious stones. Their creations illustrated events from history or legend. They also showed everyday scenes, such as peasants harvesting wheat. They depicted flowers and trees and the ideas of scientists and scholars. They indulged in fantasy, carving gargoyles and goblins, and other strange, mythical beasts. Most importantly, they used glass and stone to instruct churchgoers—most of whom could not read—in stories from the Bible. These talented craftspeople never signed their work, but the structures that they left behind tell us much about their world. As Victor Hugo, the nineteenth-century French writer, said, "In the Middle Ages, men had no great thought which they did not write in stone."

PART THREE

Merlin, the famous magician in the legend of King Arthur, dictates a story to his scribe. Many people in Eleanor's era believed in magic spells and prophecies, so they especially loved legends of Merlin.

The French and the English
in Their Own Words

Troubadour poetry began in the south of France with Eleanor's grandfather, Duke William IX of Aquitaine. Later, encouraged by Eleanor, it became France's great gift to the literature of medieval Europe. Romantic troubadour poems, inspired by ideas of courtly love and chivalry, were sung to the accompaniment of musical instruments, such as the tambourine, harp, or fiddle. Bernard de Ventadour, said to be the handsome son of an archer and a kitchen maid, was one of the most famous of the troubadours.

The best troubadours were invited to live in castles so that lords and ladies could hear poetry and music whenever they wished.

Here are three of the verses he wrote about Eleanor, whom he idolized:

When I see her, my feelings flow
Into my eyes and face; my hue
Betrays the stress I'm subject to,
I'm like a leaf when tempests blow.
So deep in love am I that tho'
A man, I'm witless as a child;
To one so hopelessly beguiled
His lady should great mercy show.

I am not one to scorn
The boon God granted me;
She said in accents clear
Before I did depart,
"Your songs they please me well."
I would each Christian soul
Could know my rapture then,
For all I write and sing
Is meant for her delight.

Lady, I'm yours and yours shall be,
Vowed to your service constantly,
This is the oath of fealty
I pledged to you this long time past.
As my first joy was all in you,
So shall my last be found there too,
So long as life in me shall last.

Sometimes troubadours' love poems angered ladies' husbands. At one point, Henry sent Bernard de Ventadour away from Eleanor's court, possibly because he sensed that the poet had truly fallen in love with his wife.

Bertran de Born was a war-loving lord of Aquitaine, as well as a poet. His poetry, unlike the courtly love verses of the romantic troubadours, was a call to—and a glorification of—war. Bertran made trouble for the Plantagenets. First he encouraged the Young King to rebel against Henry II in 1173. Then, in the 1180s, he helped stir up the Young King's jealousy of Richard. This resulted in the brothers' fighting in Aquitaine and ended with the Young King's death. Following are two of his poems in praise of battle:

> Peace delights me not!
> War—be thou my lot!
> Law—I do not know
> Save a right good blow!
>
> I care nothing for months and weeks
> For Monday or Tuesday devoted to peace,
> In April and March I do just as I will
> If enemies still remain for the kill . . .
> Peace brings me no comfort,
> I live only for war
> My belief and my thought
> Has that creed for its star.

In Germany, troubadours were called "minnesingers." Here an unknown German poet writes of Eleanor's beauty, which was talked of throughout Europe.

> The sweet young Queen
> Draws the thoughts of all upon her
> As sirens lure the witless mariners
> Upon the reef.

When Henry II imprisoned Eleanor for her role in the Great Rebellion of 1173, many of her fellow Aquitainians were deeply disturbed. Richard le Poitevin, a troubadour from Poitou who had probably known the queen since her youth, expresses his outrage below. Notice that he refers to Eleanor as the "Eagle with two heads" because she ruled over England, as well as her domain in France. The royal sons are the "eaglets," and he calls Henry the "king of the North Wind."

Tell me, Eagle with two heads . . . where were you when your eaglets, flying from their nest, dared to raise their talons against the king of the North Wind? It was you . . . who urged them to rise against their father. That is why you have been plucked from your own country and carried . . . to an alien land. . . . The king of the North Wind holds you in captivity. But do not despair; lift your voice like a bugle and it shall reach the ears of your sons. The day will come when they will set you free. . . .

Peter of Blois was a nobleman who served as royal secretary to Henry II and, later, as chancellor and secretary to Queen Eleanor. He came to know both monarchs and their children well and wrote many fascinating letters about life with the Plantagenets. In this first excerpt, Peter describes the hardships involved in traveling with the unpredictable Henry.

If the king has said he will remain in a place for a day— and particularly if he has announced his intention publicly by the mouth of a herald—he is sure to upset all the arrangements by departing early in the morning. And you see men dashing around as if they were mad, beating pack- horses, running carts into one another—in short, giving a lively imitation of Hell. If, on the other hand, the king orders an early start, he is sure to change his mind, and you can take it for granted that he will sleep until midday. Then you will see the packhorses loaded and waiting, the carts prepared, the courtiers dozing, traders fretting, and everyone grumbling. People go to ask the maids and doorkeepers what the king's plans are, for they are the only ones likely to know the secrets of the court. Many a time when the king was sleeping, a message would be passed from his chamber about a city or town he intended to go to, and . . . we would be comforted by the prospect of good lodgings. . . . But when our courtiers had gone ahead almost the whole day's ride, the king would turn aside to some other place where he had, it might be, just a single dwelling with accommodation for himself and no one else. I hardly dare say it, but I believe that in truth he took a delight in seeing what a fix he put us in. . . .

Many chronicles from the Middle Ages have survived to this day, and they give us fascinating information about life long ago. Most manuscripts were written in Latin by monks—they were among the few who could read and write—and they were often painstakingly decorated with colorful borders and illustrations like this one.

This letter of Peter's was written during the struggle between the Young King and Richard for control of Aquitaine. In it, the author strongly urges the Young King to obey his father, as Henry tries to bring about a truce. It would even have been better for the young man to have died, Peter writes, rather than having become an enemy to his father.

You establish yourself as the enemy of God and of justice, as the transgressor of all laws, if you do not heed your father, to whom you owe all that you are . . . Who offered you the stuff of existence? Your father. Who raised you? Your father. Who instructed you in weapons of war? Your father. Who put himself aside in order to make you king? Your father. Who labored in every way so that you could possess all in peace? Your father. You find nothing of which your father ought to be accused, except for the fact that he has deserved your abundant gratitude and your devotion . . . for his generosity, for his kind and lavish gifts. . . . For if God has endowed you with the span of a longer life, you will weep at an older age at what you commit in your youth; nor will there then be a place for penance, when the matter will have come to such desolation so that it cannot be repaired. . . . And would that death, which you force me to choose, had preceded these days, in which I see you as the persecutor of your father and your country; in which I look upon you as a friend to your enemies, and an enemy to friends. . . . Farewell.

In addition to being one of the greatest warriors and military strategists of his age, Richard the Lionheart was also a musician and a poet. Because of Eleanor, he absorbed the troubadour culture of Aquitaine. In this poem, which he wrote during his two-year imprisonment by Henry VI, the Holy Roman Emperor, Richard chides his friends for taking so long to raise his ransom.

I now perceive with bitter certainty,
Friend has he none who's in captivity,
Where I must lie for want of gold or fee;
I mourn myself, but more those close to me,
To whom my death a grave reproach will be—
I languish here so long.

Queen Eleanor suffered intensely, too, during Richard's captivity, for she loved him above all others. In his absence, she was trying hard to keep Philip II of France and her own son John from carving up Richard's empire. Eleanor wrote three emotional letters to Pope Celestine III, pleading with him—challenging him—to help free Richard. Here are excerpts from the first:

O holiest Pope, a cursed distance between us prevents me from speaking to you in person, but I must give vent to my grief a little, and who shall assist me with my words? I am all anxiety, both within and without and as a result my words are full of suffering. . . .

I have completely wasted away and with my flesh devoured, my bones have clung to my skin. My years pass away full of groans and I wish they could pass away altogether. . . . My insides have been torn out of me, I have lost the staff of my old age, the light of my eyes; if God assented to my prayers he would condemn my ill-fated eyes to perpetual blindness so that they no longer saw the woes of my people. . . .

King Richard is detained in chains; his brother John is killing the people of the prisoner's kingdom with the sword, he is ravaging the land with fire. In every respect the Lord has become cruel to me, turning his heavy hand against me. His anger is so against me that even my sons fight against each other. . . .

What do I do? Why do I yet live? Why do I, a wretched creature, delay? Why do I not go to see the man my soul loves, chained in beggary and iron? But doubt remains and I waver. If I go, I desert my son's kingdom, which is being plundered from every direction. . . . But if I stay, I will not see what I most want to see, the face of my son, that face which I so long for. . . .

Is your power derived from God or from men? Why then have you, so negligent, so cruel, done nothing for so long about the release of my son or is it rather that you do not dare? . . .

I am no prophetess nor the daughter of a prophet, but my grief has made many suggestions about the troubles to come, yet it also steals away the very words it suggests, for my writing is interrupted by my sobbing, my sadness saps the strength of my soul and it chokes my vocal cords with anxiety. Farewell.

Some historians believe—while others do not—that Eleanor and the highborn ladies of her court gathered in the great hall of the castle at Poitiers to hold "courts of love." Whether these courts actually took place or were instead something of a medieval fantasy or joke, Eleanor's daughter Countess Marie really did commission her chaplain, Andreas Capellanus, to write about them in a book. It is entitled *Treatise on Love and the Remedies of Love.* In it, Capellanus describes mock trials in which knights present love problems and questions about courtship to a panel of noblewomen. The panel then passes judgment on each case, guided by the principles of courtly love. The *Treatise on Love* also includes Capellanus's "Code of Love," a set of commandments regulating proper knightly behavior, such as "Thou shalt be in all things polite and courteous." Here are two of the book's "court cases," in which knights seek advice and await the ladies' rulings.

Then a question like this came up: A worthless young man and an older knight of excellent character sought the love of the same woman. The young man argued that she ought to prefer him to the older man because if he got the love he was after he might by means of it acquire an excellent character, and it would be no small credit to the woman if through her a worthless man was made into a man of good character.

To this Queen Eleanor replied as follows: "Although the young man may show that by receiving love he might rise to be a worthy man, a woman does not do very wisely if she chooses to love an unworthy man, especially when a good and . . . worthy one seeks her love. It might happen that because of the faults of the unworthy man his character

A lady gives her knight a token of her affection, possibly a circlet similar to the one she is already wearing in her hair. Thus honored, the nobleman will try to act according to the ideals of courtly love and do everything in his power to make the lady proud of him.

would not be improved even if he did receive the good things he was hoping for, since the seeds which we sow do not always produce a crop."

Another problem concerning love arises. A certain lover when fighting bravely lost an eye or some other physical adornment. He was rejected by his partner on the grounds that he was unworthy and a nuisance to her, and he was refused the customary embraces. The judgment of the lady of Narbonne goes against this woman, her reply on this case being as follows. "The woman is considered unworthy of any honor for deciding that her partner should be deprived of her love through a disfigurement occurring as the usual outcome of warfare, a thing which can happen to those who war as men should. It is the daring of men above all which usually arouses women's love and nurtures them longer in their decision to love. So why should disfigurement of limbs, arising naturally as the inevitable outcome of daring, cause a lover the loss of his love?"

In the twelfth century, there was an enthusiastic revival of the legend of King Arthur and his Knights of the Round Table. Stories about Arthur, who some historians think may have been an actual sixth-century British warrior in southwestern England, had all the elements that appealed to the medieval imagination: chivalry, courtly love, violent battle, and the magic of Merlin. One of France's great poets, Chrétien de Troyes, transformed the many tales he heard into five long poems filled with knightly adventure and highborn romance. His enormously popular works, along with those of the Welshman Geoffrey of Monmouth and the Norman Robert Wace, were largely responsible for introducing Arthurian legend into medieval literature. The legend still enchants us today.

The excerpt below is a scene from *The Knight of the Cart*, Chrétien's story about Sir Lancelot and Queen Guinevere. As you can see, the chivalrous Lancelot will do anything his queen asks, even to the point of pretending to be a coward:

Already the crowds had assembled on every side: the queen with all her ladies and the knights with their many men-at-arms. The most magnificent, the largest, and the most splendid viewing stands ever seen had been built there on the tournament field, since the queen and her ladies were to be in attendance. . . . The knights arrived by tens, by twenties, by thirties—here eighty and there ninety, a hundred or more here, two hundred there. The crowd gathered before and around the stands was so great that the combat was begun. Knights clashed whether or not they were already fully armed. There seemed to be a forest of lances. . . . Those who were to joust moved down the lists, where they encountered a great many companions with the same intent. . . . Lancelot did not participate in this first encounter; but when he did cross the meadow and the herald saw him coming on to the field, he could not refrain from shouting: "Behold the one who will take their measure! Behold the one who will take their measure!"

"Who is he?" they all asked. But the herald refused to answer.

When Lancelot entered the fray, he alone proved a match for twenty of the best. He began to do so well that no one could take their eyes from him, wherever he went. . . . [The onlookers] were all troubled by the same question: "Who is this knight who fights so well?"

The queen summoned a clever, pretty girl to her and whispered: "Damsel, you must take a message, quickly and without wasting words. Hurry down from these stands and go at once to that knight bearing the red shield; tell him in secret that I bid him 'do his worst.'"

The girl swiftly and discreetly did as the queen asked. She hurried after the knight until she was near enough to tell him in a voice that no one could overhear: "Sir, my lady the queen bids me tell you to 'do your worst.'"

The moment he heard her, Lancelot said that he would gladly do so, as one who wishes only to please the queen. Then he set out against a knight as fast as his horse would carry him, but when he should have struck him, he missed.

From this moment until dark he did the worst he could, because it was the queen's pleasure. The other knight, attacking him in turn, did not miss, but struck Lancelot such a powerful blow that Lancelot wheeled and fled and did not turn his horse against any knight during the rest of that day. He would rather die than do anything unless he were sure that it would bring him shame, disgrace, and dishonor, and he pretended to be afraid of all those who approached him. The knights who had praised him before now laughed and joked at his expense. And the herald, who used to say, "This one will beat them all, one after another!" was very dispirited and embarrassed at becoming the butt of the knights' gibes.

Opposite: King Arthur and Queen Guinevere sit at a banquet table while Sir Lancelot kneels before them. Long after Eleanor's reign, Lancelot was considered the greatest of all the Knights of the Round Table. He was the perfect embodiment of bravery and gentleness, chivalry and courtly love.

Geoffrey of Monmouth was a medieval chronicler whose book *History of the Kings of Britain* includes a collection of legends about King Arthur. Some of the prophecies of Arthur's sorcerer, Merlin, were thought to predict the destinies of Eleanor, Henry II, and their sons. Here is a prediction that twelfth-century people believed applied to Eleanor:

> *The eagle of the broken pledge shall rejoice in her third nestling.*

Another chronicler of the time, Ralph of Diceto, explains Merlin's prophecy in this way:

> *Indeed she was called "eagle" since she spread her wings over two kingdoms, that of the French and of the English. But she was separated from the French king because of blood relationship and removed by the English king through confinement in prison, which continued for sixteen years. Thus on both sides she was called "Eagle of the broken pledge." However, you can thus understand what was added: "She will rejoice in her third nestling." Richard, the third son, or third nestling, intended to elevate his mother's name.*

Henry II, like Eleanor and Richard, was buried at the abbey church of Fontevrault. The stone effigy placed on his tomb wears

The stone effigy on the tomb of Henry II

a crown and holds a king's scepter. Here is Henry's poignant epitaph:

> I am Henry the King. To me
> Divers realms were subject.
> I was duke and count of many provinces.
> Eight feet of ground is now enough for me,
> Whom many kingdoms failed to satisfy.
> Who reads these lines, let him reflect
> Upon the narrowness of death,
> And in my case behold
> The image of our mortal lot.
> This scanty tomb doth now suffice
> For whom the Earth was not enough.

And this is what the nuns at Fontevrault, with whom Eleanor spent her last years, wrote about their queen:

She enhanced the grandeur of her birth by the honesty of her life, the purity of her morals, the flower of her virtues; and in the conduct of her blameless life, she surpassed almost all the queens of the world.

Glossary

abbey: A monastery, containing a home and a church for a community of monks or nuns.

abbot: The leading church official of an abbey for men.

annul: To cancel or undo.

archbishop: The highest rank of bishop.

baron: A nobleman who is the vassal of a high-ranking lord.

chancellor: The English king's secretary, or high-level administrator.

chivalry: The knights' code of service to God, lord, and lady.

county: A province ruled by a nobleman called a count.

crossbow: A bow that is held horizontally and shoots a very powerful bolt, or arrow.

Crusade: A military expedition launched by medieval Christians to take control of the Middle Eastern region they called the Holy Land.

duchy: A province ruled by a nobleman called a duke.

dynasty: A series of rulers who belong to the same family.

effigy: The sculpted representation of a person, often on his or her tomb.

epitaph: The inscription on a gravestone or tomb.

feudal: Having to do with the political and military system in which medieval landowners granted portions of their land to other men, in exchange for military service.

fief: A territory granted by a lord and held under feudal obligations.

flying buttresses: Stone supports that are connected to the outside wall of a building in order to help hold it up.

Gothic: A style of architecture that began in the twelfth century, noted for its pointed arches and stained-glass windows.

homage: The ceremony in which a vassal declares his loyalty to his lord.

joust: A medieval sport in which two armed knights seek to knock each other off their horses.

manuscript: A book written by hand; medieval manuscripts were often illustrated with colorful paintings called miniatures or illuminations.

overlord: A feudal lord, usually a king, with authority over all other lords in a region.

prelate: A high-ranking church official, such as an abbot or bishop.

quest: A search or mission that takes on great spiritual or emotional importance.

radical: Very different from the views that are held by the majority of people at a given time.

regent: One who rules in place of an absent king or queen.

scribe: A person who writes down or copies letters, books, or other written materials.

troubadour: A type of medieval poet-musician whose romantic themes were chivalry and courtly love and who often lived in the courts of noblemen or monarchs.

vassal: A person who was granted land (a fief) by a lord and held it in exchange for feudal obligations.

To Learn More about the Middle Ages

BOOKS

Fiction

Crossley-Holland, Kevin. *The Seeing Stone.* New York: Scholastic, 2000.

Konigsburg, E. L. *A Proud Taste for Scarlet and Miniver.* New York: Atheneum, 1973.

Malory, Sir Thomas. *King Arthur.* New York: Dodd, Mead & Company, 1953.

Sutcliff, Rosemary. *The Sword and the Circle.* New York: E. P. Dutton, 1981.

White, T. H. *The Book of Merlyn.* Austin and London: University of Texas Press, 1977.

White, T. H. *The Once and Future King.* New York: G. P. Putnam's Sons, 2002.

Nonfiction

Hinds, Kathryn. Life in the Middle Ages series: *The Castle, The Church, The City, The Countryside.* New York: Benchmark Books, 2001.

Macaulay, David. *Castle.* Boston: Houghton Mifflin Company, 1977.

Macaulay, David. *Cathedral: The Story of Its Construction.* Boston: Houghton Mifflin Company, 1973.

FILM

Goldman, James. *The Lion in Winter.* VHS. Directed by Anthony Harvey. An Embassy Pictures release: 1968 Haworth Productions Ltd. and 1987 Embassy Home Entertainment.

MUSEUMS

The Cloisters Museum, Fort Tryon Park, New York, New York.

The Metropolitan Museum of Art, 1000 Fifth Avenue, New York,
New York.

ONLINE INFORMATION

www.learner.org/exhibits/middleages
This is an excellent site that offers links to many topics related to
life in the Middle Ages, including feudalism, the Crusades, the art
of the period, knights and heraldry, as well as a tour of an imaginary
medieval castle.

Bibliography

Bartlett, Robert, ed. *Medieval Panorama.* Los Angeles: J. Paul Getty Museum Publications, 2001.

Benton, Janetta Rebold. *Art of the Middle Ages* (World of Art series). London: Thames and Hudson, 2002.

Bishop, Morris. *The Middle Ages.* New York: Houghton Mifflin, 2001.

Brooks, Polly Schoyer, and Nancy Zinsser Walworth. *The World of Walls: The Middle Ages in Western Europe.* Philadelphia: J. B. Lippincott, 1966.

Capellanus, Andreas. *The Art of Courtly Love.* Translated by John Jay Parry. New York: Frederick Ungar, 1959.

Caswell, Caroline, trans. *Patrologia Latina* database. Alexandria, VA: Chadwyck-Healey, 1995.

Chamberlin, E. R. *Life in Medieval France.* London: B. T. Batsford, 1967.

Chrétien de Troyes. *Arthurian Romances.* Translated by William W. Kibler. London: Penguin Books, 1991.

Crawford, Anne, ed. *Letters of the Queens of England.* Gloucestershire: Sutton Publishing Limited, 1994.

Fry, Plantagenet Somerset. *The Kings and Queens of England and Scotland.* New York: Dorling Kindersley, 1990.

Hartman, Gertrude. *Medieval Days and Ways.* New York: Macmillan, 1937.

Heer, Friedrich. *The Medieval World: Europe 1100–1350.* Cleveland and New York: World, 1961.

Holmes, George, ed. *The Oxford Illustrated History of Medieval Europe.* Oxford: Oxford University Press, 1988.

Jaeger, Stephen C. *Origins of Courtliness: Civilizing Trends and the Formation of Courtly Ideals, 939–1210* (Middle Ages series). Philadelphia: University of Pennsylvania Press, 2000.

Kelly, Amy. *Eleanor of Aquitaine and the Four Kings.* Cambridge, MA: Harvard University Press, 1950.

Map, Walter. *Courtiers' Trifles.* Edited and translated by M. R. James. Oxford: Clarendon Press, 1983.

Meade, Marion. *Eleanor of Aquitaine: A Biography.* New York: Penguin Books, 1991.

Mills, Dorothy. *The Middle Ages.* New York: G. P. Putnam's Sons, 1935.

Pernoud, Regine. *Eleanor of Aquitaine.* New York: Coward-McCann, 1967.

Peters, Edward. *Europe and the Middle Ages.* 4th ed. Upper Saddle River, NJ: Prentice Hall, 2003.

Quennell, Marjorie. *A History of Everyday Things in England, 1066–1799.* New York: Charles Scribner's Sons, 1941.

Rowling, Marjorie. *Everyday Life in Medieval Times.* London: B. T. Batsford, 1968.

Severy, Merle, ed. *The Age of Chivalry.* Washington, D.C.: National Geographic Society, 1969.

Staines, David, trans. *The Complete Romances of Chrétien de Troyes.* Bloomington and Indianapolis: Indiana University Press, 1990.

Stubbs, William, ed. *Opera Historica: The Historical Works of Master Ralph de Diceto, Dean of London.* London: Longman & Co., 1876.

Walsh, P. G. *Andreas Capellanus on Love.* London: Gerald Duckworth & Co. Ltd., 1993.

Warren, W. L. *Henry II.* Berkeley and Los Angeles: University of California Press, 1973.

Weir, Alison. *Eleanor of Aquitaine.* New York: Ballantine Books, 1999.

Notes

Part One: Eleanor, the Queen

p. 4 "I thought to have married": Kelly, *Eleanor of Aquitaine and the Four Kings*, p. 77.

p. 6 "a very evil woman": Meade, *Eleanor of Aquitaine*, p. 110.

p. 6 "gracious, lovely": Meade, *Eleanor of Aquitaine*, p. 160.

p. 11 "sweet as nectar": Pernoud, *Eleanor of Aquitaine*, p. 16.

p. 13 "with abundance of all delights": Weir, *Eleanor of Aquitaine*, p. 15.

p. 13 "lively": Kelly, *Eleanor of Aquitaine and the Four Kings*, p. 6.

p. 13 "charming": Kelly, *Eleanor of Aquitaine and the Four Kings*, p. 6.

p. 16 "To Jerusalem!": Severy, *The Age of Chivalry*, p. 241.

p. 19 "their horses' hooves trod": Weir, *Eleanor of Aquitaine*, p. 61.

p. 20 "loved the queen passionately": Meade, *Eleanor of Aquitaine*, p. 125.

p. 21 "lesser sex": Meade, *Eleanor of Aquitaine*, p. 3.

p. 23 "lovely eyes": Meade, *Eleanor of Aquitaine*, p. 160.

p. 23 "breath of paradise": Kelly, *Eleanor of Aquitaine and the Four Kings*, p. 86.

p. 25 "Henry the Peacemaker": Weir, *Eleanor of Aquitaine*, p. 103.

p. 25 "seems rather to come": Kelly, *Eleanor of Aquitaine and the Four Kings*, p. 177.

p. 26 "Eleanor, by the Grace": Weir, *Eleanor of Aquitaine*, p. 127.

p. 27 "The King and Becket": Meade, *Eleanor of Aquitaine*, p. 175.

p. 28 "honor of God": Meade, *Eleanor of Aquitaine*, p. 245.

p. 28 "Aren't you the son": Meade, *Eleanor of Aquitaine*, p. 220.

p. 30 "Who will rid me": Weir, *Eleanor of Aquitaine*, p. 186.

p. 34 "obedient in all things": Meade, *Eleanor of Aquitaine*, p. 253.

p. 34 "had understanding in matters": Kelly, *Eleanor of Aquitaine and the Four Kings*, p. 85.

p. 34 "what dawn is": Kelly, *Eleanor of Aquitaine and the Four Kings*, p. 100.

p. 35 "Beware your wife": Weir, *Eleanor of Aquitaine*, p. 199.

p. 35 "lord of little land": Kelly, *Eleanor of Aquitaine and the Four Kings*, p. 206.

p. 36 "War was in his heart": Kelly, *Eleanor of Aquitaine and the Four Kings*, p. 215.

p. 36 "threw himself upon the ground": Meade, *Eleanor of Aquitaine*, p. 289.

p. 37 "From the devil": Brooks, *The World of Walls*, p. 119.

p. 38 "My whole body is on fire": Weir, *Eleanor of Aquitaine*, p. 245.

p. 38 "Say no more": Meade, *Eleanor of Aquitaine*, p. 299.

p. 38 "Shame, shame": Weir, *Eleanor of Aquitaine*, p. 246.

p. 38 "the great one": Weir, *Eleanor of Aquitaine*, p. 193.

p. 38 "great wisdom": Weir, *Eleanor of Aquitaine*, p. 281.

p. 38 "exceedingly respected": Weir, *Eleanor of Aquitaine*, p. 281.

p. 39 "The Earth trembled": Kelly, *Eleanor of Aquitaine and the Four Kings*, p. 256.

p. 40 "Evil Richard": Weir, *Eleanor of Aquitaine*, p. 268.

p. 41 "torment": Weir, *Eleanor of Aquitaine*, p. 284.

p. 41 "I long for death": Meade, *Eleanor of Aquitaine*, p. 322.

p. 41 "the staff of my old age": Weir, *Eleanor of Aquitaine*, p. 313.

p. 42 "light-minded": Meade, *Eleanor of Aquitaine*, p. 325.

p. 44 "I have been very ill": Weir, *Eleanor of Aquitaine*, p. 330.

Part Two: Everyday Life in Eleanor's Realm

Part Three: The French and the English in Their Own Words

Index

Page numbers for illustrations are in **boldface**.

About the Author

"Knights in armor, gloomy castles bristling with towers, cathedrals in which light from stained-glass windows pierces the shadows, court ladies in veils and fur-trimmed robes—the Middle Ages have always seemed so mysterious and faraway to me. Yet the more I learned about Eleanor's time, the more I realized that quite a few medieval customs, laws, and beliefs are still with us today. And the more I wondered about Eleanor of Aquitaine. Although she lived eight hundred years ago, she was in many ways a 'modern' woman. There is enough that is fascinating about her century to fill a lifetime of reading."

In addition to *Eleanor of Aquitaine and the High Middle Ages*, Nancy Plain has written four other nonfiction books for young people. Her biography of the American artist Mary Cassatt was a 1995 selection for the New York Public Library's list of Books for the Teen Age, and her book *Louis XVI, Marie Antoinette and the French Revolution* was named a Notable Social Studies Trade Book for Young People, 2002. The author has three grown daughters and lives in New Jersey with her husband and her dog Molly.